Shoestring Press

POENA DAMNI

Z213: EXIT

POENA DAMNI
Z213: EXIT
DIMITRIS LYACOS

ISBN: 978-1-910323-62-5

PUBLISHED BY Shoestring Press, Nottingham 2016.

PRINTED BY ImprintDigital, Upton Pyne, Exeter, Devon EX5 5HY
www.imprint.co.uk // info@imprintdigital.com

COVER DESIGN, ARTWORK AND LAYOUT FOR THE PRESENT EDITION:
Dominik Ziller // *Hauptstadtbureau*

First English Edition, translated by Shorsha Sullivan,
published by Shoestring Press, Nottingham 2010.
ISBN: 978-1-907356-05-6

TITLE OF THE ORIGINAL:
Poena Damni, Z213: ΕΞΟΔΟΣ. Typothito, Athens 2009.

BY THE SAME AUTHOR:

- *Poena Damni, With the People from the Bridge.*
  Translated by Shorsha Sullivan. Shoestring Press,
  Nottingham 2014.

- *Poena Damni, The First Death.*
  Translated by Shorsha Sullivan. With six masks by Friedrich
  Unegg. Shoestring Press, Nottingham, 2000.

DIMITRIS LYACOS

POENA DAMNI
Z213: EXIT

Second Revised Edition
Translated by Shorsha Sullivan

Shoestring Press

For Menis Lefoussis

Z213: EXIT

10
11

these names and that's how they found me. And as soon as they brought me I stayed for a while and then they took me it was a building of four wards large yards and rooms the rest of the people were there four wards separate not far from the sea. And we would eat together sometimes and in the middle a log with cut branches on top over it an opening for the smoke, and ashes spread out on the floor black stains and ashes. And from the pores in the walls a little water would come and sometimes you could ask go upstairs and visit somebody else and when sometimes in the evening the power was out and we were sitting silent in the dark   but the wards which weren't connected   three four five among us fond of each other yet most of us there would die at some point all of us me too and then those who believed used to cry out others did not that right we had and we were in all those wards about a thousand and each day a man from personnel would come with a list and stand in the doorway right there in the entrance the main door to go in standing and shouting to them to come out and they would call them then take them from there and remained ten somewhere else fifteen depending on ward and they would take them to a special place from the evening of the day before and next day in the morning they would come and take them from there and you could hear at that time they were going in and calling their names hear those now saying goodbye to us we were about two thousand. And they were saying goodbye to us now I with all the others saying goodbye to us and the place sounding with their goodbyes. And then they would come out go into a car and round the back there was the sea and they were going. And as soon as they would come out you could hear now people shouting and from that place in a car from the back to the sea it was not very far it was from the back where they dug pits and sometimes

12
13

the water would reach there and the town was woken by this noise. And they would lower them down into the pit. This is what comes to my mind most of the time. And to hear them cry as far as the last houses of the town where the wall was and everybody understood. And some used to get close to the pits and go back again and it wasn't a secret it was under our feet but nobody. A whole town just about. And that moment indescribable moment when I went down past midnight and saw bringing them in that truck down to the sea.

If I could, only from that place he told me about, that gallery which leads behind the wall to the abandoned fort and the tunnel through the mountain. Because all other roads were guarded to prevent anyone getting through. Lights overhead broken apart from one at the far end. And then that skylight, an open hole in the dark. Going inside that way you leave the city behind, the passage which narrows and narrows, you go up, hear sudden flutterings. Hear like a river flowing somewhere around. Soon you make out the end, light, you come up trees drizzle, leaves spilled at your feet. Voices and footsteps draw near then away. Then you start going down again as fast as you can, get there before break of day. More would die tomorrow. And some will know about you. Night cut in two by the yellow strip running through it. And he had told you to wait for the time they come and the way out is easier. And about fetching and separating them, two ranks – two ranks mingling together as they were pushing them forward. And many were falling into the sea or stumbling and the rest trampling on them. And I wore the cross like he had told me and passed by the side of the tower and came out on the road for the station. From there you could leave. If I could take a train from there. But I sat down then to recover for I was in pain.

16
17

I got up, wandered about quite a while, then walked to the first platform on the other side. A soldier beside a niche in the wall laid on his side, eyes shut, a blanket over his legs, a pile of clothes beside him – uniforms – a kit-bag behind his back. I went, pulled out a pair of trousers and a jacket, eyes shut, a little blood under his nose, he raised his head gently, wiped it off with his sleeve. I returned to the toilets to change, came back left my clothes on the heap. Eyes closed, a drop of blood under his nose. I looked for a pair of boots from the kit-bag and put them on there, sat down beside him. Bent double, his side on the half-empty sleeve. A red beam held us inside it for a while and went away again. It must have been already past six. Cold, keeping my hands under my armpits, something hard, the little Bible in the pocket, I open the pages blank here and there a few notes, somewhere else parts written clumped together, could not make them out. It had almost got dark. I sat still for a while waiting for what – stood up, walked again, to the clock, the time-table, evening service 21.13. In one and a half hours.

18
19

Even if it didn't make a great difference in the compartment, at least to some extent. Turned off the light, pulled the curtain, passed a strap hanging there two or three times as tightly as I could around the door handle in case someone came. Sat for a little, no one, went out again walked up and down the corridor, no one, lit a cigarette, it would be nearly time. Went in again tied up waited inside, a jolt in the dark, another one after that in about five minutes when we set off, one more cigarette, laid down, better now. As if I were awake and as if I were sleeping, suddenly something beside me, inside me, awake, asleep, dark changing landscape, day breaks, you turn your back to the light. We stopped, early morning, a little water from the tap in the toilet, then outside. Blue, and around the slopes of the hills. Old border post. Someone came out told us to get on again, same man came up to do the check, the papers were fine. I got off once more and got a sandwich – bread and beef – from a roadside vendor. Frozen hard. First light that opens your lungs all around and above and from here onwards the strong smell of the landscape goes with you all along.

20
21

A few hours more, station, deserted, a dirt road leading into the town, mud, mud, blankets outside, mouldering corrugated houses, the shattered pylon further behind, not even a car, rubbish, two children setting fire to a heap, two or three other fires on the horizon, houses, the smell even more acid, tarmac pieces and pieces, concrete block houses, few people, half-open doors, half-light, the mattress as if it were soaked, that milk, the cramp in the stomach and dizziness, when I awoke, I hurried to make it before it got dark, a little by chance and from what I remembered, asked questions, the other side, back to the bridge, murmur of water, trees turning black but I could still see, it was in front of me almost as soon as I entered. What are you doing here, sit for a while beside you, if you could also back then, did someone bend over, hear you while still you were heard, your eyes that were gleaming, eyes growing dim, pain growing dim, with how many more did they bring you, the bell, silence as they lowered you down, stifled song and a pause, murmur of water. I am cold, I walk away through other names, photos that look at you and yet they cannot, the sun now again at its end. On the road back, on the plain, a tepid, breath, like the last, and a gleam, the river falling behind, the town mute as before, with some wine on the end of a table, the Bible being erased, between its pages the words of a stranger, among his pieces I write wherever I find a no-man's land.

22
23

As long as a match stays alight. As much as you have time to see in the room that flares and fizzles out. The images holding, briefly, then fall. Some lines you manage, they are gone, another match, again. Pieces missing, empty pages, match, again. An alien sentence comes and sticks in your mind. And where are the dwelling places of the wicked. Ask those who walk by your side. Match, some smudged parts again like those of the testament, then some of his pieces, then mine. The light lasts so little time that you can hardly manage to write, in the dark you can't see if the page is blank. You write, a match, words falling on top of each other, another page, write, again a match, page blank, continue, another half-written page, read, the matches almost gone. You turn the pages by feel, finger them. Where you find written patches, you add your own beneath, you write in between. A match, read, your own together with the stranger's, more again. As if you were speaking with someone. Match, pull on the cigarette try to read under the glow. No. Match, fear that the objects go away again. As when I went away.

                                        Paths were all being
guarded so that no one can get through.

And thrown out now on the roads I have opened myself, I shall be bound by them.

There were more that escaped before dawn.

Without bond or limit, witnesses, precious.

A special subdivision of the Peregrini is constituted by the stateless. (Peregrini Dedicitii)

24
25

who although considered free

If I go out on the road I might be able to find

as belonging to no country.

Last match.
Full Moon
    hung on the tree   dry
the light at the window
                        sorts out

the forest to the west

laughter, ours –   best medicine

        to arm

hands unable to hold anymore

drunk

                                        Of the
high tide   the shadows

                    Suddenly drums bursting out
                    pick up and go don't know where

                    and silence   fear

                                        frightened, like a child

                                                    humiliated
                                                    before them

                                        couldn't hold out

                                                    graves

                        don't stop digging he said

                                                    the village

                                                    the funerals

burying them during the night

when I'm back

a day   together

28
29

grow old

within a day
                        at the fringes of the fire

we encountered many

who plunged

                        their breast

                        we found
butter eggs in the   bread honey and later

were giving their daughters in marriage that day

and then were falling with a crash into

stalks that we cut and ate just ra

of the ash

30
31

and in the

                       a glow of twilight around it and fire

flashing like lightning

mouths

Aesk – heyl – hopa (The hope of salvation is found in the wood, the demons rush out from the wood, or something like that)

Didn't find any, came back. I don't remember how long nor where from. Dawn broke again.

32
33

Tell those who were waiting not to wait none of us will return. The sky is leaving again, the newspapers rot in the corridor, the same trees pass again darker before us, those who wrench the doors looking for a place, who are coming in at the next stop. The light outside cutting the evening to pieces, harsh evenings that fall among strangers, the story shatters within you, pieces, fading away in the ebb of this time, the one dissolving into the other before you manage to sleep. And the snail hurries to go back on its tracks, a tale you remember unfinished, wrinkles that still hold a colour on memory's transient seed, birds that awake the dew on their wings and you leave with them into the all-white frozen sky, but you wake and are baked again. Not fever, remembrance of sorrow exhausts you don't know why, before you are well awake and the barren feeling comes back again to your hands, the rest suddenly fades away at once, you are one recollection a broken box emptying, after the tempest this calm, you search for support, get up like an old man, feel cold, remember birds' wings, magistrates' sticks decorated with feathers the bones of an angel, sink again images and words monotone prayer.

34
35

with cotton wool or toilet paper which crammed your mouth, soaks up your saliva, you are scarcely able to breathe. But mainly you are thirsty, this wakes you up and the glass beside you empty. Night still but what time, you will get up to ask for some water, the carriage deserted, farther back, drops on the window, you wet your hand to wet your mouth, further still further back the carriage deserted, and one more, shudder, like voices that swell, a carriage of voices. They give you water. Their animals sleep at the back, they ask you questions you sit among them. You drink water again. Laughter, voices ask you, you are about to say something but you feel dizzy. A piece of meat from hand to hand, you go and lie down at the side, they give you food, a bottle from hand to hand, wine, a circle further back singing, the others between the animals sleep. Dark faces, voices fraying in bitter carnival, their heads, changing animal heads, the lamb's body ends in the head of a man with eyes shut. They put someone between two windows and he raises his hands, tall and broad, they bind him by the wrists to the bars, left right. Lamb's head, they put on his head the skin from its flayed head. They speak to him. He sings. Slow, disjointed song. Dark cross of the man as day breaks. They dress him in a blue garment, beside you someone was turning a torch on and off from joy from emotion tears had come to their eyes. Alien joy of children, your smile joins them for a while, and then as if someone had gagged you but you calm down again and breathe freely. And they were showing the livid scars on their faces, victories that had conquered the world, our faith, they were saying and our body one body in Him, you could hear them sing, it won't be long until the day comes, the season will change. Around you all red. And outside, along the view of the river beating up to the windows, slower now the train in its bend, and wherever they could, all together, a closing circle, the native women struggling to climb aboard.

36
37

38
39

Lorries pouring tons of mud mounting up. Sm
coffee, boiled in a pot, they gave me a cup, you ans
persistent words with your hands, you don't know
Outside the window the river like sending out lig
within, blinding you. Your eyelids with all the weig
line of the horizon. Blurs. A wave spreading out of
with nowhere to cling to turning back and cascading
expanses of snow. The workmen of a gang raising a
and building. Bridges, one almost finished. To the cr
the mountain out of control and shuddering upwards

Wine again. Every so often they would fill up, once
washed the eyes of the cross of the lamb that was look
around. Fumbling its body and singing. Look at the ho
in his palms. Nail your finger inside, call out the blood, th
were singing. And something like: the crosses, the crosses,
them go deep. With rhythms that made you dizzy again, i
the slow whirl of the light growing stronger, in the carriag
spinning round with you.

The slow bells from the church which must be near me I stopped for a while and waited and now they were chiming again. And I entered and sat down there and like stains below, the slabs as if blooded. Who was there ringing, guesses confused not made clear, who was there ringing the bell waves going down the dome, the echo of water that creeps up on it and drips inside here. And the flashes right in through the windows from one to the next like a searchlight turning around seeking me out. Here, in a flooded pit full of bodies, branches that cover and float leaves that float on faces unknown funerary gifts on the side, like his words and the Writ that mix on this page, then a line standing out on its own

fr en p lms b rn ng.

frozen palms burning. Gestures of the walls that invite you. A hole high up opposite, you can hold on to the ivy shoots climb up and see where exactly you are. You don't care, those traces cling to you now, people that brought here a chunk of the life they lived, pushed it as far as this place, same like you, came here and stayed together, like those leaves, those leaves that came in where from you don't know, a pile that gathers in front of the saints, them joined together as well, one by the other, side by side, gaze on the people that kneel, a circle, that will protect them for now. But, release, and what's left, spent mouths leaving again away from those arches that covered them and they dream still for a while of courtyards where souls find rest, a flower brigade of angels awaiting them there.

40
41

And then the illusion dries up and it is an empty uninhabited house. The icons behind the colour that changes, same shape, same face painted again all around. And there, in the corner, the body demolished, like metal plates inside it, until dark falls completely, leaning out from the last fading saint, his face pressing lips tight.

42
43

go and free the girl from her hollowed chamber

take her up ·

come with us, let us lay wait for blood

well-ordered among us you

lined up twelve

that you had called unto you   whose names are

                              and more around you, a great
crowd on the ripples stray leaves from an autumnal

circling around you
            of a theatre.

And rusted cymbals behind the gate past feasts
of a life   in the cupboard
oil in a bottle
like milk and   who were those here perhaps

at night they gather here where from

where do they come from

Look how their bodies are growing under the

POENA DAMNI

44
45

you reach out to the wall your hand touches their flesh - their flesh is a bed standing upright behind them.

The web getting thicker, the spider climbing inside.

You can still see the shells she has emptied, her empty bed trembling

hanging down from a thread that shall never break.

She shall still stand for a while ahead of those faces around her. She will go again,

behind the icons again

be

be

God.

His mild cold eyes
she who you entered

now is around me   you sprinkle the soil with
fruit, eyelids with vinegar, our cities with blood

secret cities   secretly born
secretly mated   hav hot eyes of an
adulteress

warm   church

when did he ever
when did he sleep
who is with me inside here really, who

and the painted bodies will ben
                         kindly faces to face
only now I know

            fall asleep here
                 their vanes dilating above me as if it were
your dress

God was wrapped up in there frozen
expressionless   you would say there were thousands
of eyes together

all the   crosses
silver windmills on top
grind from

48
49

below white caterpillars and dust
Inside the

into your breast they have not passed however

If I were to hold some of the bread they had given me and
a little meat too

That train was going out of the zone, remember what they
told you
Something about the exile's

Why do you always clasp your stomach just as you go to sleep

The saint over your head.
Horseman with spear in his hands hanging over you, as if
holding a flute. A flute-player painted with fingers
emaciated sewing the mouth of the monster. Round the
back paths go up to the rock a tree, this too made out of
stone, the ivy that on her lips   and
climbs
into the most fertile God climbs,

roofs further behind, the country they were talking about

After the nightfall
sleep,
all around her one bed, still coming there
a new nest, your spider inside there weaving
her eyes your eyes mild still cold when

you share out his body, one piece each
incandescent   steeped in the fire

POENA DAMNI

50
51

bouquets of thyme

and the dirge below
the crowd, they lift him up
candles in hand

twelve of the
                    bastions and the men behind them
                                        in war

52
53

.I think of you but not the way I used to. My eyes open in sleep, a hand seizes me. And the sweetness of somebody's touch. I am falling, and the same dream again the chest of a child that a woman holds in her arms. Lips on it, wet, blood-soaked her lips. I start upright. The others are sleeping. Days walking uphill, view of an evergreen plateau, stay there. Quiet. When only the wounded mumble close to your ear.

I took something that made me get over my fears and then I wouldn't care about anything. I did not care about anything, a knife cut my finger, and I didn't care about stopping the blood. Nothing to stay for. Daybreak of a dawn without light. And around one side and the other monasteries empty nests and a whole crowd out there, a river between. And there was a crowd. They are singing.

the bridal chambers are filled
in the heavens
there is a multitude of waters
in the heavens

Below bodies the stream sweeps along, on the bank a row of them thrown face upwards, I run around like a madman looking for you, a woman presses her daughter to her, poor, we haven't eaten for days. Gleam without hope still gleaming. In dreams jostling the one into my other. Like then a boy on top of his mother, help me lift her up he was holding her, tight by her soaked rags, have you got matches strike one, it is dark. Shows me the black avenues and a door at the end. My name that I saw written on it. First time I felt this kind of pain, like a bite. I saw, yet another soldier fallen nearby. Tears in his eyes, cried out where are you. Could not see, dark from the mud that covered his eyes, don't drink from this water, couldn't hear, the march past blanked it out. And it was the memorial they were chanting for us. On our backs, above us the poplars all round. For the lost, country and youth we had lost. For the horses rolling in blood. And then their carcasses rest under

54
55

the olive trees. When the sacrifice starts and they pour something over. Where are you. And they are all gone, here are only the gods that take off their jackets and give us cover. Dead holding on to images scattered until they too fade forever away. And I see the others, do not go near let them get up by themselves. Like the bare ramrod hitting you in the stomach, a saw, an empty canteen. I recall. New Year's Eve. My stomach in knots. Sleeping beside me who. As if he were whispering an answer to me. Now it grows dark again. I am a child, I encounter the gypsy. Who takes by day to the roads and sings. In distant villages in the cemeteries for alms. They said he was dead. And during Carnival in the squares roaming about. Comes and asks us to light a cigarette for him. A knot deep down, memory, poor girl. Working all night, ruffling through uniforms. In the cloakroom of travelling players should you find something to change into. Your face fading again, I wish I could hold your head for a while, and your body is warm and when you are bending to kiss me you hesitate as if you listen out for the sound of them coming. Or the sound of water or wooden fingers on drums. Beside me late flowers on your mouth and this is your kiss. The eve of the lights, do you remember? On the day itself I dig into the stone wall and bury my knife there. I left after that. Last time I saw you.

In the wood, I saw it there, on a fir tree. Hanging from the tree.

the body shall not remain all night upon the tree

for he is accursed   he that is hanged on a tree

Pharmak

56
57

And he shall take

the lot fell on it to be a scapegoat and

shall present it alive

and shall send it away into the wilderness.

58
59

Cruel the evening again in the station and the train and another station, silent, and the train tail of an animal moving ahead, and another station alien eyes not looking yet you want to hide again, a long narrow passage that flows away in the rain and covers you. Sitting still you cannot your thoughts cannot help you stand up you can neither go forwards nor backwards. Socks wet, take off your shoes, no, still, you stay, almost as to go out of the world, lights passing by, nothing but lights for you, nothing exists behind this. No thought triggers your body not even pain. One by one all those that fled all those you left, pieces, pieces like ice breaking and falling in front of your feet. And it melts before you can move. The rhythm of the metal draws you with it a shadow out in the corridor lighting a cigarette the same tree that has passed before you a thousand times. You smoke one as well. You take off shoes and socks lie down. Cramp in the stomach, the usual. You cover your legs with the pullover, lie face down. Chilly berth that sticks on your face. You wear the pullover, under the jacket you put the Bible for a pillow. Her breast, her half-opened mouth. Some life. You unbutton your trousers put your hand in. A hand that holds you a body you stretched on top of. She is coming close almost you touch her and she is gone again, saliva, pale light and the listless pulse of the body powerless almost. You hold your breath, her breasts come, you press hard, comes inside you, from inside you squeeze as many drops as you can, from inside you. Stay still, calm, empty, darkness is hiding you, afterwards sleep. A jolt, you slip all but fall you put out your arm, palm on the floor, a crumpled book open, take it, take a look at the cover: The First Death. You leaf through it for a while, then this too for a pillow, on top of the Bible. When you wake again two bodies entwined, the flesh between them in pieces, that melt, breast onto breast, that fade one into the other, fading out when you decide to stand up.

POENA DAMNI

**60
61**

Make a point of remembering to write as much as I can. As much as I remember. In order for me to remember. As I keep writing I go into it again. Afterwards it is as if it were not I. How do I know that I have written this. Faded, someone else's words. My own handwriting though. From a void I wake up within, time after time. Nights following one after the other behind me. Women in black that shout and push on the platform try to get on almost blindly in a way that you can't manage getting off. Waves beating black spit in your face waves going to break one pushing the other apprehensive of a catastrophe somewhere. A boy held my hand as he got in. Palm red on which the blood had scarcely dried. Wanted to take hold of something. On the angry red skin cut open blood stealthily hides inside for a while then runs again. Later, alone, the strip that led me right here from the station, when I turned round to look if the sea were behind me a grey strip out there then a rather more yellowish grey and always a little more yellow right up to here. Right up to here where walls enter the sides of the mountain falling away, the afternoon grows dark as you enter. Black dirt and yellow rocks that shine and waste away in your hands. A landing, you climb a little higher, look into the empty cistern, clods you break off from the walls crumbling into your hands, what else could you expect. Later on, cautiously on the mouldering planks, you follow conveyor belts, from one to the next, a small door further inside, perhaps this is what you have been looking for. Traces of people. Seated around a stool pensive gold miners play cards, their hands' shadows exchanging then fading, hidden again in the dark. And after that stones, yellow, gleam, stones that light up, matches flare again in the room. Then someone takes out and reads to them, something, a poem. Silence. Silence. As if he were chanting. And something else. From the poet's pocket one more paper, he reads to them. The others that listen yaw

62
63

they lean on each other. How early they sleep.
Heavy breathing that grows louder in sleep odies   one
after the other before you in rows. Of dreams. Later nobody
anywhere, just yellow mud. The cupboard torn shirts dust
dust a stool four or five chairs, shelf, an empty flower pot.
The light that returns to the wall etched again and again like
a poem   n a   blind going deeper every day, until the
end. A race of blind rats. Deeper, each day they are burrow-
ing deeper. Straight ahead! Backwards, forwards, as far as
the range one single breath would allow, as deep as they can,
one breath further in, hole getting deeper, weave the web
further, as much as their strength would allow, now air com-
ing in, you fall into another gallery's mouth, a little more
still and you are out.

Outside again

                    foot-hill chimneys

my eyes get accustomed take a breath gaze at the sea they
are restored horizon and more from that side turbulent

            wind without them beating their wings. Flock.
Seagulls. From the sky, a bit darker now.

Enter again, galleries engulfing the mountain, conveyor
belts leading you right to the bottom the galleries getting
narrower

POENA DAMNI

64
65

Fir   a   mat   mud as you keep digging
softer warmer a hand statue hand broken drawing you in-
wards among the others. Incorruptible bodies.

Even as stone and iron. Statues. Rotting wooden ladder, you
climb up a white scrap a torn garment, no, a torn seagull
among the clothes round about before they seize them in
their claws. New bodies. Rats' dens. The beams horizontal
crosses on the roof upri
around the walls broken
jawbone and tee from   oxous. Empty cavities, funnels
going still deeper.

And those who would raid the city what would they find to
take from this place. Only the shadows of those who used
to roam around the corridors between these shafts. And
then going home one after the other. Mute.

Wagons transporting dirty hands and torn shirts, rocks
crumbling from walls like old masks.

I turned back and follow again a gallery leading to another
room. As if it were a lorry passing by overhead, I feel it from
the vibrations on the broken corrugated iron, rumbling
drawing away like a distant earthquake fading out. Over-
head.

66
67

Still going. I follow a rail. Straight ahead. Num bers on en-
trances on both sides of the track. Props. Like a huge hour-
glass. I had seen it before. Well maybe before, I think I have
been here before. A hole in the roof. Draught. A beat once
more overhead like someone approaching. Like those foot-
steps when I was there. Someone coming for us. At night as
we were lying

Mist, when I used to go out from the side with the beach.
Looking away as far as I could.

Of demons' necks stretched on high.
And then again in the dark of the dormitories.

This beat again coming behind me, slowly. Broken slabs. My
footsteps' echo. A hand as if from a statue. Smashed under
my feet. Some bird trapped in here. Maybe rats. Could be,
here in the hollows. Statues of rats in the holes. That sound
of footsteps again. The echo. I sit down. Silence. Silence. That
sound again. Now behind me. Who.

68
69

There is nothing there. Pulleys. Gear-wheels, you turn them full circle. One circle turning another. And another further ahead. Rusted but you could still turn them around. Played a little with it. A chain going down deep in the dark.

How deep. This way.

Why do you stand and look up to heaven.

Why do you stand and look upwards. You can see, you are able to reckon how far you have come down but there's no way you can climb up from that place.

Not that deep, not entirely dark. You get used to it. Going down for now but I will go up after that. Light sputters and water comes in. I am lucky to be inside with this storm. I rest in a spot where I see almost nothing but I can hear

I still have the flashlight he gave me.

Heavy rain   waking you up. You see a stream on your side coming down from above. Follow it and get out.

You go up to a point, a chute blocked by the rubble, take out a couple of stones, take out some more, mud underneath, for the most part. Earth crumbling as you put your arm through the hole.

70
71

You had seen a shovel on your way here, go back and take it.

It isn't a shovel, looks more like a paddle. Broken timber, big bottles, a bucket of something like tar, on the side a wheel-barrow.

Take it and try. Start digging on top.

You are tired. You can go back and search and try to remember which way you entered.

Can't remember. Go back and dig.

That much is enough for you to crawl through. Tight squeeze but you can do it.
You must be getting closer now to the shaft. Light, stark, a beam watching over you. Getting stronger and stronger as you ascend.

Empty hole watching you from below, full hole watching you from above, like an eye giving off light.

Dig for the light with your hands. A door that has rotted. Break it, dig deeper in there.

You climb up on all fours stop start again, see roots hanging above you like ropes. You are getting there. You want to dig faster your hands are hurting you now you don't

72
73

Wind cleansing your eyes. You catch your breath, don't see, only breathe the world overhead, you are cold, you enter a niche for a while to warm up a little. You hear the wind, those that were hiding follow behind you, you hear them, you ask them to tell you but they can't open their mouths. You would give them to drink if you had.

And the wor st as a jet of water on them as if worm by the wood.

Leads down again you are afraid it might take you deeper in there. You are sweating, can't breathe, as if the room were shrinking around you.

light, urgently calls you to climb calls you drops before you

You are out. Hill, a little under the top. Sun, rest under the sun. Shivering world. Across the fields the red yellow

one tree leaning over the other – a bridge not too far away – animals leaning over each other

lying down together

You will spend the night here. It will get dark in a while.

I woke in the middle of the night. Two great fires burning

And burned   like a flaming fire, which devoureth
round about

even though by the most favourable calculations we will have re-
turned before next week. A lot of smoke still and our eyes smarting

cries and laments and we approached out of curiosity

                          and I heard and then in my grief I wept and
I prayed in anguish and when the sun had set I saw
being baptized   fireproof in fire
of forests

the sea of burnt trunks, heaps, one on top of the other

that I will n   forget

POENA DAMNI

76
77

What was there. Narrow shafts and their houses on top. That's why they had dug the whole place underneath otherwise they would have killed them if they had found them. You almost still feel them that's why at some point I thought that someone was looking at me, that someone else was in there apart from myself. And a room like a church and another a kitchen and it smelled as if he were still there, I smelled his food. And this big room with those big eggs like tables, tipped on the side and like green hairs on top. Let me sleep now. Tomorrow I will go down and go to the station. If it won't come tomorrow I must spend the night over there.

78
79

to here. Warmth, see people around talking again. You don't care what about, only hear them talk. Petrol. Stove. I had missed it, warmth and wait for a drink. My turn, not yet. He talks looks at you as if you were with them. My turn. Not yet. Talks about some journey, a few days elsewhere, back again. Petrol, when you swallow you slightly feel it right up your throat. You swallow again. Speaks, changes the piece, speaks. Drink coming your way, you drink and listen to him look at him, long, grey, curly. Yellowred, and the grey colour outside looking more like blue. It brings you comfort, drinking, sitting in there, all together, including those across, all together around you. Still living here. Seven, nine, nine and you. And him coming in with the cake. Candles, her snuffing them, they laugh, she brings a piece for you too, the rails fresh from the rain, too late now for a train. You drink, it brings you comfort. One more. She smiles, touches your shoulder, a fleeting shudder, she asks if you are cold. You look at her mouth. And when am I going to go away again. Toilet comes first. Stay there for a while. By yourself. River in time of peace. Dark moths like holes on the wall, who are they waiting for, who will be hiding inside them until dawn comes until they go home to sleep. Somewhere that no one can see them, deep inside the crack on the opposite wall, inch by inch growing over us here. And the curtains like winding sheets waiting. Outside the wind blows. Win dpro of. The rain is not going to stop. She called him to come. A crate of beer, coming. Take a bottle and drink the world forming inside it, that takes gradual shape while you keep drinking on, and yet, in the end, it is too heavy for you, you cannot keep it up any longer, you drop it and it shatters again. Drink, and then everything back again falling in place apart from this one, piece from the cake, left over odd piece doesn't fit anywhere stays in your hand. Taste it. Wake with it. The rails parallel roots long

80
81

narrow train gardens wet and the rigging runs parallel to their sky. Inside you something. Beneath the breath of sadness something as if. Inside me. Music that slowly. Lifting you up. I had forgotten how. A beam of light will fill your head and you'll remember what's been said. People, necks one leaning over the other waiting for what. Animals with the knife hanging over their head. That looks like you that looks like me. And those galleries in n ether darkness how did I come out. Tracking without traces of those searching for me of those I seek. One more. The voltage sags for a while the screen signal is lost, black and white, coloured, black and white, wave on the opposite wall. Of a storm. Without voice m ind if there is music that covers. The lights fail for a while, only a while, a piece covers, you drink, mutter je creuserai la terre jusqu'apres ma mort pour couvrir ton corps d'or et de lumiere to cover your body devenir l'ombre de ton ombre l'ombre de ton chien, rain, you drink again, rain. Send a raven to check if it has dried up somewhere. Prelude for what is awaiting you, their lips following on. Should music stop we would be suddenly heard. Chorus of stutterers. If she were to kiss me. Like the, for months I would watch him chiselling in the rock a face with a hammer. The rock that was his, the face that was hers. Striking. Like pleading. Striking on the face. Comes again, one more on the house. Getting a little more blue outside, sat there, perhaps it might lay its eggs in that crevice. Her breasts behind my shoulder, cigarette, I still have some left. You think that, what if you kissed her, your stomach feels tight, the music that

your chest feels tight your body asking for more. That I could be in love with almost everyone, I think that people are the greatest fun
and I will be

When did I last listen to it. Jester.

Just give me a chance to do my turn for you.   Lying together

82
83

but in the grey of the morning
my mind becomes confused
between the dead and the sleeping

Morning, only with what's left inside you and it's yours.
Now it presses and needs to come out

iss

84
85

the sun leaves the station chases you, goes up, moves in front of you, find where you had stayed, search, there or some place else, on the grey facades that do not recognise you, what do you remember of the road that is lost, turn back to a corner sit down a while, and once again, the roads you are changing, hours that you wander, old women looking at you through the window grow larger grow smaller you walk without coming out anywhere, the roads grow wider narrower bend beneath your feet rise go up again, you get up sit go a bit further, ask someone, enter, church crowded, did somebody die, you rest a little, closed knees, eyes closed, remember something go out again, others along with you, the bell, the door unlocking porter, you enter behind them to the end of the corridor, then on the right and up the staircase, thick glasses, and a red stain under his nose, he paid no attention to you or took you for someone else, how could he make you out him looking from the light into the dark, or he doesn't see well, go up the stairs, to the top, lie down, cover yourself, it is still too early to sleep. You are cold, cover yourself, you snuggle down, tremble, stretch out, from feet to body to hands a clammy fluid covers you, he took you for someone else and let you in, who else lives here, it covers you, you awake in a dream, empty, eyes that open and separate us again, you cannot pull her to you, you get up, you fall, you are thirsty, you wake up for water, many times the same story, what time is it, the lights outside, count how many on how many off, the plaster tired above waiting, like a cockroach, alone and still like a cockroach, searching here and there for a warm spot to hide in, you sweat, from the heat, the roof comes down to your feet the window comes down to your feet, from there what can you see, only sky, sky without anything, nothing over the roofs, from your feet right up to your knees, you get up go out into the corridor, the other rooms empty as well, apart from where sleep can be heard, you go back to your bed eyes open into the dark you wait in the dark in order to sleep.

Days there.

I went out only to get something to eat, two or three times.

Once he was not there, once he did not notice me.

        to go for a walk.

Next time he smiled as if he had recognised me.

Bone-pits beside the houses

Further on fires had started up.

I go out in the evening and walk about. Sneaking out, I slip away
and I am lost in the streets

and I wait for the fires to start up again
sit around
        They were burning the life boa
ch nts

Crowd in the streets. Songs like prayers.
Midnight on Good Friday.

and I break a little bread in my soup. My hands tremble.

every evening, in the houses still smouldering,
altarpieces
        that lived through the Resurrection, till it burned
them down

broken and they threw those too on the heap

88
89

And when in passing I walk up the pavement behind

                     with the good luck they had and were saved.

Such a crowd
pressing together on the wharfs
at the distant ships' drone

they were jumping without minding the distance

                    under the ruins of the towers, and when we ap-
proached

I try to stay awake. I douse my face in water, I press

Rotting flags.

A little water on my lips.

You would think they weren't human

with full light, and all the people saw the thunderings and the light-
nings, and the noise of the trumpet, and the mountain smoking

badly wounded and he was babbling

about those who walked through the sea that had opened and those
chasing them taken by waves and turned into seagulls, they are the
seagulls he once used to see he

90
91

half obliterated by rust, half sunken:

Ulysses

outside the hotel   Exce sior
some ten,
calling you to go up
thirty
come, come

a story about Circes' bed,
make nests   to deposit
their eggs there

drops of blood   and if thou wilt make me an altar of stone
to

                      corporal from

Time of departure: two thirteen

                again the foot. I have no painkiller

92
93

And when you can no longer remember, just meaningless things here and there, and you can't. But still try even then, as the twilight sets in, stand and look at the past, walk again along the corridors where your eyes used to wander, watchful ghosts, open the boxes, think of the other side of the wall. Sit at the side of the road and see yourself pass. See the web, see how the passages of the maze all lead again to the same point which does not exactly coincide with the exit.

94
95

We went up. A staircase behind the toilets, vertical almost, I could scarcely see anything else, followed almost blindly. Like a wave rearing, a gasp. As if it were not real until we went in and she closed the door. Chair, bed, didn't see anything else, they clustered about me. She drew the curtain, the bed yielded, the chair to hold my trousers for a while. Half-open mouth. Half-open mouth above me. She took me I sat next to her leant back she came on top opened took my hand and put it in to grope among her breasts. Her hand in between parting the hairs. I raised myself a little to touch her, fell back again, her mouth on me. She was sucking too strongly, the chair, wherever I could, fasten my eyes, everything blurred and dissolved, couldn't hold on, I was closing my eyes to hold myself together inside, not even from there, she was sucking too strongly, too fast, nothing, I couldn't, nothing would come. She was breathing out, her breath between my legs. I couldn't see outside. The curtain that she had drawn across the skylight. Wave standing. She sat, worked her hand up and down on me. I thought I had seen an extra finger on the underside of her palm. Strongly, too strongly. She was hurting me. I tried to keep my eyes on her mouth. I could no more, stood up. Her hand on me, I sat again at her side, she started again, with her hand beating and squeezing, my hand wandering on breasts heavy without nipples belly without navel. Lips I was fixing my gaze on, I leant back our tongues touched. Something was about to come out, then nothing. Wave standing. A shadow behind, his shadow, the dread that he had followed me here. He will knock on the door, open it, he will find me half-naked, standing upright in front of the bed. She was still stroking her hand up and down on me. The bell that was heard outside, that was chiming for us. Empty between these strokes, nothing coming out from inside. Without her managing to draw anything out of me. She got up, drew the curtain. No one.

96
97

I went down again into the street. After that I don't remember. Only that I woke up, with a knock on the door in the middle of the night, clutching sperm and saliva from her mouth.

98
99

Where did I come from? My name? Where was I heading? Sit, if I wanted to sit for a while. Relax, I'd been walking for long without purpose before coming in, I was afraid to try again. Should she lower the light or better like this? Not to take off her clothes. Myself to lie down and her to sit on my lap so that I could look at her. As I had imagined her the night before when she had come out to the window. I wanted her then. Voices from the street or the other rooms, laughter. Trousers carefully on the chair. Why would she need it, the napkin? I laid back with my legs stretched out together, arms glued to my body. Like in a coffin. And I stopped breathing for a while. But better if I kept breathing, calmly and a little slower. She began, I turned my eyes up to the ceiling. White, a blank sheet two yards above us. She asked me if I wanted slow or faster, I couldn't sense, told her a bit slower. It felt as though an alien member was stuck to my body. An alien member coming out of my body. Back to front, like cleaning the barrel of a gun. Front to back, now slower somewhat. Her breasts were pressing forward. I lifted my back up and down again, that's better, slowly, then a little faster. She was looking down at her hand, waiting attentively. I could feel it was squeezing me and then open-ing and relaxing. I was feeling it squeeze the blood in my veins, more and more strongly, could not understand how. I just wanted to see her moving on top. No, not yet, for a moment, only the mirror, the white wall again, the hard body on me. For a moment you don't look anywhere, just feel, the body fills out, saliva starting in the mouth, the animal scratches inside and wants to get out, you want to get out, the animal thirsty pushes inside to exit your mind overflowing. Overflowing between her fingers and surging and you move towards her breasts. And then, then as if you didn't exist, as if the animal died and me that I came wholly inside her. If I could stay like this, empty, empty and clean.

100
101

Then the world stands calmly ahead, peaceful, simple, clean beneath your eyes. Then it would, would not matter however alone I might be. She smiled as if she knew, I would go away, would come back, would want her again, now I am thinking of her, if only again. She took the napkin she wiped me. And she pressed it on top for a while, like over a pimple that's burst.

102
103

Who are they preparing again for tonight? The scum of
                                                    the morning

outside the doors, drained heap, arms and legs
as if of statues, half-covered in mud,
and they wait, how could they go (hollow and rotten
boats swallow them to nowhere,

to nowhere joined together, with the smell of the earth
                                            closing
above, their good hope shut down again). And the
rest in a train where to, from a world that was,
until they arrive to where, far, where you can't feel,
                                            nothing
reaches your ears your nose,

only fear. And suspicions, sidelong glances tiredness,
each one a bodiless wing. Beating up in the mind one by one
and together, squalls of sea-corpses, hooves of iron
                                            horses
sunken wheels, chains that sprout from the mud,
a friend at your side that weeps. And yet

in these cavities, light from ruined arms gleam
like a candle as once in those country churches of
Christians, amassing coffins around them. These are
the very ones now buried, naked, and their bodies have
                                            rotted
quicker now, without cries and grief

POENA DAMNI

104
105

and delay. And yet those steps are heard at midday,
songs, death that sings through the womb of
your mother, through the women that strive to rise up
from the clay. Or hide it under their tongues, like
a secret, which if you had known you would not have
                                        returned.

And yet the mind always returns to the places it will not
                                        return,
it grows faint, I grew faint with all that on my mind, in the
                                        end
this bit does not fit anywhere, me, the head
sagging, the road going backwards across the window
                                the astonishment that
you still stand, as the pale lights outside were making me
                                        drowsy,

needles injecting straight into the eyes. And yet, I understand
                                        that
the road runs also inside me, I see, as if it were eagles
                                        that
had come down over the ruins stooping, chests open
over the lungs, hearts, withered
lost. And your brother at your side to weep.

Remember that old story no more, let go, it has already
                                        sunk
enough, that world behind you will not emerge again
                                from the dark
already died, no eyes to look upwards, no head
to peep out from the shell. Just a bone
that reminded you of something, but not for long any
                                        more.

106
107

We left behind us this harbour as well, now we approach,
                                        the sea
already appeared the rock of the burnt out Lighthouse they were
telling you of
I am now far away, yet I still think of you for a while that –
you, your cities exhausted, the aged

children, the aching teeth of desire, the carriages full of
the drowned, the truth that tightens, around what
                                        happened it tightens,
you say it, they gather together, a circle, the gallows, the
                                        trees,
the fruit that does not fall on the ground, the bodies that
                                        broke from affection,
the friend you don't see and don't hear,

look still that beside you

108
109

In the beginning you don't see only imagine, then you think that you see – you lay out in your mind a space where, yet, nothing is visible. Mere space and fog. Then you isolate one part of it and try to make out the landscape in your field of vision, to the point that, one by one, objects can be discerned. But the farther away you look it gets blurry again and as you are moving ahead limits are moving away. Then you look out of the window beside you, a few yards away and you are seeing them travel, it isn't yourself, it's the objects, if objects you can call them. You see them depart at the side of the train, you can't touch them, you see them. In sequence, one after the other. And even if your eyes were closed they would still travel through touch, if you could lay out your arm and touch them, you would feel them go past your hand, encounters in time that follow each other in sequence. That's how you would call it, sequence, and if you were to make in reverse the same movement, you would be able to predict, the same sequence, from the end to the beginning. And if you would like to start somewhere else you could change the course, change that sequence. Your hand from your trousers, to the chair, and its arm, to the glass in the window, and back again, same sequence with the gaps you had noticed in space. It is you that, all those, you are calling them objects, they are only names, however, that speak to the soul. And you have always the option to close your eyes and start afresh, it's the same again, you know how it is. Not like when you look, and, gradually, you perceive them to be otherwise, changing colour because light changes, grow bigger when you are bringing them close, until you can see nothing more, they vanish, they come in and out of the light. You forget them into the dark and wait for them in the light. And now that we are going ahead in the dark you look and expect to find out what will emerge out of there, as we keep going. For you know as well that the sky is there, even though it is dark,

110
111

even though empty. As you know that the earth beneath is pushing you forward. The wheel pushes it and, in its turn, it pushes it forward. If it were to yield a little we would be going down inside it. Perhaps we are heading somewhere in order to go down. Perhaps when we get there, on the horizon, this surface won't be so hard after all. We are heading there all together, with the train shifting the light and playing with it, the light shifting and playing over a thing that is stealing away. That changes form, a surface in motion. And the road opens, as we approach the road opens up a new road, for us not to be forced to a stop, a door is constantly opening in front of us. We shall never find it in front of us closed, shall never stop, never knock, no one will open for us. We shall never take hold of the skein uncoiling. It will coil and uncoil its edges before us, we will keep seeing it, a dark sign far away ahead. Noiselessly, or traveling with the train of this noise. That pulls you or pushes, you move but stay still there. And you don't care any more how you will manage to open and enter and see something else because even if you advance you will not reach anything, there is no outside and inside, you never came in, for you only the entrance is there, you follow a door that is constantly opening, you are not inside however, and, of course, there is no way you can get out.

112
113

And I heard the groan and someone that, that told me: walk. Walk in the midst of the sea, and I shall save you and do not stop until you reach the other side. And someone else who said: and you shall take our bones with you. And I rested a while, and I saw in the sky a long narrow cloud. And it stood still all day and all night. And at night as if it would catch fire and the sea red. Red. And I pondered why I had roamed here and who was coming after me. And perhaps he will catch me up at the edge of the sea. And I was afraid. I could have stayed there, die and not travel. Perhaps they left me in order to see what I would do and then send someone after me. Perhaps better in there than dying alone here. And someone that said again: walk and be saved, and take a rod, and stretch your hand over the sea and let the rod fall and rip it in two. And pass along in the middle. And the cloud came and stood behind me and it got dark again. And I took the rod, and stretched my hand out over the sea, and the wind was blowing all night, two winds in opposing directions from the same point. And the sea was gathered together a heap on one side and a heap on the other. And a road between. And I passed then in between, on one side and on the other the red wall. And I heard the groan behind me again and remembered how they were bringing them in the truck down to the beach. And I heard, the voices again, that why, and the reed in the wind beating.

114
115

He spake   I will pursue I will overtake thee
I will glut my soul   of the flesh   they melted all.
Saddle on bloodied waves
covered them

                    whisper.

Ere it   will be night   let us chant to
in the giving

they bear fruit   as hoar frost on the ground
barks of hounds on the scent

          Wood, and they had cast it into the water
and it was made sweet
but left it until morning. And
It bred worms and stank   in the bottom

          full bowls and they could not drink

and dissolved all except one. And the bones under the sun like gypsum

and he set off out of the desert

passages   and encamped there.
Grant us   arms stretching out to the water

                    make us gods which shall go before us

shipwreck of the   under the mount.

116
117

Nobody is coming after me. Surely they have forgotten about me. Nobody will ever come here to find me. He will never be able to find me. Nobody ever. And when I fled they didn't even realise. They took no notice of me no one cared no one remembers. Now they will remember neither when nor how. Not even I. Tracks only, a hazy memory and those images when I look at what I have written, tracks of footprints in the mud before it starts raining again. Uncertain images of the road and thoughts mumbled words, and if you read them without the names you won't understand, it could have been anywhere, and then I spoke with no one and those who saw me no chance that they remember me. Every so often a face seeming familiar, from another time, someone looked at you, you recognised him, no, a part of another on a stranger's face. Or the rhythm of the steps that sound behind you, the rhythm of your own steps, which occasionally you think follow you, they stop when you stop, or for a moment you think he is coming behind you, or you think that someone is breathing behind the door and will now come in. And then nothing, and then back again, and you suddenly turn your head as if you had heard him. But no one. You are far away, no one knows you, no one wants to find you, no one is looking for you. And tomorrow you will be somewhere else still farther away, still more difficult yet, even if they would send someone. But they don't know the way and before they find out you have decamped somewhere else. They know how to search but they don't know what way. And even if they set off from somewhere they will still be quite far. And they will not be many. Perhaps just one. One is like all of them together. Same eyes that search, same mind that calculates the next move. Same legs that run same arms that spread wide. Ears straining to listen, nostrils over their prey. Always acted like that. Two eyes, two ears, two nostrils, two arms, two legs. The symmetry of the machine that pursues you.

118
119

A net that thinks decides and moves ahead. The head a fish-hook the body a belt. All the same. Me too. One behind the other. Forward back further back, to follow the road. And even if you don't know you run ahead anyway, because someone is always coming behind you. Sooner or later he comes. And sometimes there comes a hand taking you by the shoulder, or a worm that climbs up on your hand. It rolls on a pillow of saliva. Forward. And as it rolls it is growing and wrapping around you. A flat tongue on its saliva with two eyes that rise up to peer at you. Maybe not you, they check for a confortable place to start from. Like him that, that night we were hungry, that had etched an open mouth on his stomach. Likewise this tongue is also stomach and mouth, always open. From there you go somewhere else, on the inner road opening up, in the twists of the gut, there of course you are unconscious by now, unconscious you take the road of return and when you wake up they have brought you inside there again.

120
121

Password: Track brake, end of route here

with fear. I try to pull the trigger, my hand as if
paralysed
                Tattered posters   And face.   The architect of
the plan. The houses collapsed all
around

    Remnants of the very last attack.

                              of reason.

spider's web   summer.

You beat a retreat not orderly. Of the remainder some with thirst
oppressed, others forespent of breath

we searched and found nothing and they were telling me why have
you brought us here to die, give us water to drink

                                          that

I be held
responsible for the failure of the operation

        and you take the field across, pitch tents and the others are
near us, across, and they watch us and wait for the right time
            right to the utmost bounds of our endurance,

they said the same things again,   bent pipe or broken,
tomorrow they will dig up the line

122
123

but without my feeling the pain

with some   probably we will still remain here
several days.

and I rise up and lead you by day in a column of cloud and at night
in a column of fire

it is possible that they take us somewhere else.

that I go on at length with all this, but you should know what the
situation is like over here and especially
but if it's about   and not

I weave paths of perdition and the earth has swallowed them and
they have sunk like lead in turbulent water

            Nor   all night he was telling me how the barrel
is
            rifled and the wormgear for adjustment

and the wakefulness necessary.
photograph on the marble   the only woman we
saw here and
                                a chain
of explosions, in the

124
125

like an archipelago in the deepest darkness and we rudderless
and of others

guard until blinding of the sleepless eyes

You can sit and draw up as many plans as you wish but what is the
point
you think some train will pass if you manage to get as far as there
And the others over the ruin expect from you

of the freedom which will be a burden to you, you would roam alone
here and there with no one to   no-
body will come and seek
the price   of your wasted life
breath   for ignora nt

carcasses those too will wear away in your mind and you will not
remember in the end

              with   hoarseness he called it,
from crying out and from what we were breathing.

and some haemoptyses

feelings of hope, love, or compassion, for nobody, nothing, empty, as
if we had left it all there

And if you still live through it as if it were always like that

126
127

you always find the other way
that is eating you up, of the secret you don't want to talk about, who
could listen

        come to take

and I will come, your hand, how is your hand

I will leave it I cannot take it with me

You cannot come here to see me of course, but next month we shall
be rather
what I am writing to you while I am still here.
        perhaps   us to sit and
you would mend the fire that had gone out, the damp dripping logs,
like when we used to sit and drink, all together until morning

The ardour of the dwellers on earth behold I cast out before your
eyes

And when everything comes to an end   I shall fill
the sleeping-bag wet and dirty and shall leave again with

                        And the men took that present and they took
double money in their hands

your legs alien as you drag them,

128
129

And let us be lost, perhaps better for us like that.

like charred coins in glass cases,

                              whatever you can afford on behalf
of the

the blood that gathers scattered brushstrokes on the still body
                              The eyes of his father
bending above him, do you remember

to the sparrows   and to the rusty
wires in the periwinkles
and the colour of the sky the same day and night

We found an oil drum. In the back, lime-wash half way up, with
difficulty I kept them from drinking
                              of the pigeons from their
neck and they were sucking the blood

and the glow and the sweet scent of the burnt sacrifice
before the Lord

follow line straight ahead

130
131

You sleep at night. At night you wake up. Not even the shadow of a tree, a sign, something standing upright. Desert. Sand. Like you they are sleeping. Night. Every time you get up you expect daybreak, it is night, you sleep wake up it is night. That continues many days while you are travelling. As if you were pursuing a light which recedes with the speed you advance. For days it is like this. Then it dawns a little, a little. A line on the horizon, light, sky or sand or ash, more light, you do not know where from, goes on for a couple of hours, then again night. And then all over again, you can no longer keep count how long does it last either the day or the night or the light. At first, each day almost the same then shorter and shorter, in the end it seems to you that the sun rises and sets within a few minutes. As if time fading out as if nothing perishing here. Day like a train moving in front of your own, waits a little, then slips away ahead. You just about hear the whistle ahead like wind that goes through a pipe. And while you sleep you don't know what happens either, what could have been changed while you have been sleeping. If things are different when you woke up just now, it could have been different before and you might not have remembered. Or if it is the same, the scenery, one way or the other you don't see much of it. Or, it could be that you do not remember this, something else you remember, you sleep, you wake up so many times, so often, you don't know when you are asleep and when you are awake, why be awake, now you may be asleep, what you remember you may remember in sleep, wake up in a dream, remember inside a dream, different memory other things you remember when you are in a dream, you have a different life in the dream, you remember who you are what you did, and even though you may not be the person you were when again you wake up you don't doubt who you are in the dream, even when you are changing and you are changing continuously, you

132
133

don't wonder, things are naturally so, it is not strange, you are changing continuously, your body, around you, everything everywhere, you are somebody else, but you are the same, you are him. This is continuity, you travel, perhaps in your mind, a paper world real, God reeling up and down landscapes and buildings, knocks down, opens new roads, doesn't like it, changes again, but there isn't a seam, His world is onefold, and you perceive neither seam nor contradiction, continuity only. An injection you have forgotten at once, a skin slowly settling over what you remembered, they change, all things, memory changes, you change yourself, some woman you search for, you don't know if you were seeking another, if you had some other hope, some other aim. Tomorrow perhaps something else might erase those things as well, the new veil of the world, but you will never know it, you won't be able to know it. What have you done, if it is indeed what you remember. Who is to tell you. Or even your story to now. Or if the name, the one you are hiding, if it's a name at the end of a series of names.

Anyway, if I can think of myself right here, there ought to be something else outside, some place else. Now, if this outside is part of my mind, my mind then is not made of one single piece, it isn't onefold, there's here and there's there, outside and inside, that is to say, in a way, there is something in it that is outside of myself. Something outside of myself. Somewhere else. Even if I don't know where this happens to be, where i am myself, where I happen to be on the map, which place is here, which is elsewhere. Thought by itself tells you. Even if it is all otherwise and I don't rightly remember, even if all things around me are fake. I am here, I am not there: two worlds alien to each other. And then, the space, distance, the road, even if I didn't travel myself. The road exists.

134
135

It began with something like drowsiness. I could see what was happening but could not move, not even open my mouth. Not even think about simple things, where, what day or what time. I was not sure. In a confusion I couldn't shake off. I was very hot. I wanted to take off my clothes. I lowered my trousers. There was someone stretched out beside me, fallen down, I wanted to piss on him as he was fallen there. I went and kept trying but nothing would come.

Could be from something in the food, could be from something we had inhaled. But nothing smelled bad. I was beginning to see in a blur. Mouth completely dry. Suddenly my heart was beating louder and faster. Skin burning and growing red. Burning. We were madly thirsty. And a weakness and arms and legs not to obey and not to coordinate.

Two letters the second Z, I think, and then some numbers. Why do I remember this? I don't even remember where I saw them written. Could be simply the way they had divided us, the section perhaps and number of people in there. I crawled to a corner and was looking around. And then, every so often a fear suddenly seizing me I don't remember why. I was looking and at first couldn't believe it

And came out, he, of a manhole cursing and had burst into laughter. And then took a stone for a pillow and fell down and slept at my side. And like a tooth that was sprouting from his head. And the sun went down red and giving off smoke. And we slept. And we woke and a beam of light a ladder that was coming down from the clouds down to the earth. And it had like feet, as it were, braced on the earth and a head in the sky. And they were going up and down on it. And they were going up and down on it, angels with the faces of

136
137

our own. And behind me he said: don't be afraid. And angels were going up and down. Don't be afraid, because I will protect you on your road

And he said, you go up and you go down and when you are down your own are burning and your memories and you don't want to leave them. Everything will burn to the end, you suffer, but nobody is punishing you, they are just setting your soul free. Don't be afraid, because while you fear death they will rend your soul like demons. Only calm down and you will see the angels who are setting you free and then you will be free. And he took the stone and poured oil on top.

surely, they were taking them so as not to kill them in front of us. Bringing, taking. Then my own turn. Days came and went and they were staring at me eye to eye. Panic. I was sleeping deeply and when I was up I could not understand again where I was, I was crawling further away and looking about, I was waking from one place to the other, I was waking, was waking, was waking, I couldn't remember, I could, later as if nothing had happened, but like a lie slowly fading and coming again. Exhaustion.

138
139

Doesn't write properly, almost run out.
Line that sets off and fades away.
One colour, not earth, nor horizon, nor sky.
Looking into an empty bottle.
A straight line, without any twists, steady.
Motionless on the circles of the wheels carrying you.
The evening will come.
Bushes, very scattered.
Like snow or salt, not so white, more like the sand.
Stop, get out.
No one else either in front or behind.
Motionless train in a hole in the map.
What you remember is not, now forget it. What you wrote.
Or other marks, or his own parts that you have been reading.
Not even the Scripture stands out, very sparse, like the bushes.
Call, to see if someone will hear you.
And if they would find me what would they make of me.
I won't care, I am not afraid as before.
The engine cut off too, nothing is heard.
I am hungry and the cold is getting to me.
Newspaper inside for whatever heat it may keep.
I press and play my finger on my stomach and it rustles.
I was writing down when do I sleep and when do I wake up
to distinguish the days for myself.
Here nobody sleeps neither wakes, nor light comes from
anywhere.
You cannot know how long all that lasts.
You continue to write because you still hope, almost.
Some thing living on.
Apart from yourself.
Place.
Place where the world empties.
An opening or place or house of God on the earth,
an opening or Gateway without interior side without entrance.

While it still stands before you don't speak and don't think.
It is the end of the line but you are not ready, you will leave
and come back again.
Turn back and get on the train.
And hush and write only what you see and what you hear.
From here on only what you see and what you hear.
About yourself nothing more, hush about yourself.
The pain will finally pass, you will get out.
Fall down and worship but think nothing.
Fall on your knees and empty yourself.
And wait only to hear.
Started, the engine again.

142
143

The bottle of blood and a sketch of where I should come down and the way I should go next. I took it along as he had asked me, half-full just above midway. So that it doesn't show, in a black bag. It had clotted since yesterday. Before I went to bed I had placed it beside me, I woke up, thirsty and would almost have drunk, it was like water on top. Drunk, I had stretched out a blanket they gave me and crashed the way I was. We had been chatting, we had eaten and then I was singing along with them, around the lamb, at first one of them carving then they all fell on it together. First they reached for each other and all joined hands and then we began to eat and drink all together down on the ground. We would now and then throw a log on the fire to keep it going. As it was being roasted most of them were sitting around, now and again they would change places at the spit, someone else would take over, a hungry band feasting. Camp in the town's remains their children scrambling on the rubble playing searching. A circle, wine, laughter, teasing, old stories, a story about someone setting up a play from the gospel with a dead woman waking up in a car and a tormented madman that goes with her so that he can manage to sleep. Go see them, a crowd gathers, at the next station, under the bridge. Take, give him this bottle as well, this one is on me. It's over there on the edge of the pit where we butchered. He was the one who had filled it from the lamb's blood, in the beginning had first let it run, a basin then underneath when the pressure eased off, in the end what was left, back into the pit which blackened and drank. Left aside on the spot pelt and all, they had called me to hold on while they were skinning it first with the knife near the tail, then on the fat, then arm all the way inside the animal right up over the elbow, as if putting a sleeve on, then again a bit with the knife, and again. And then a cut to the stomach up to the rib. The arm then inside again, up to the elbow again to detach it entirely, like a coat

144
145

taken off it and laid aside. Then scraping the body a bit with the knife and swilling it with the hose. And then from inside, he drew out the offal still hot and handed it over to be prepared. It was bleating very loudly and struggling hard when they had turned it on its back, until the knife fell and it went limp, only the hind legs twitched a little. Its cry rousing the place as they were escorting it. Almost as soon as I got there, I had just sat down on the side watching them throw food to it and cutting off a few hairs from its head after it stooped down - you would think they had been waiting for me in order to make a start.

146
147

from an animal, armed, that is being followed, that is seeking you out, get away by day, by night you sleep, less, get away, get away do not stop when you know he is approaching, stand for a while, get away still until you are tired, and once more, again, get away always, but feel he is coming, as time goes by he is approaching, and still now that the distance increases, and now that you draw away still the distance decreases, you are drowsy, every so often his shadow closes your eyes, you open them, you move on, it's blocking your throat, you get tired more easily, always more often, you don't have the strength, you look behind and expect him, you get away again, you are drowsy, you close your eyes, you see him before you, you get away you are tired, mostly you stand, you close your eyes open them see him again, you don't want to go any further, you shall sink to your knees, tiredness hurts even more, you are less afraid, you are feeling the blow, you open your mouth, you look at his mouth, you don't want to stand up any more.

TRANSLATOR'S NOTE
Two different fonts appear in this edition, in line with the two different fonts
of the Greek text. Old and New Testament excerpts as well as excerpts from
other ancient Greek sources are embedded in various places within the
"lighter font" text. To render biblical excerpts in English I have followed
The King James Version.

ACKNOWLEDGEMENTS

Over the years that I have been occupied with this translation Gregory Solomon has patiently read and re-read my drafts and has offered a variety of precious comments. I am also indebted to Paul B. Roth, poet and publisher of The Bitter Oleander Press whose acute suggestions were important for this new, revised version.

This translation is dedicated to the memory of my beloved wife Anne.